DISNEY · PIXAR

TOY STORY

BOOK 12
Long
Vowels

PHONICS
READING PROGRAM

Long-Vowels Activity Book

ISBN: 978-1-338-57295-7

10 9 8 7 6 5 4 3 2 1   19 20 21 22 23

Printed in Malaysia   106

First printing, 2019

Book design by Marissa Asuncion

Scholastic Inc.

Long Vowels

There are 26 letters in the alphabet. Five letters are vowels. They are **a**, **e**, **i**, **o**, and **u**. Each long-vowel sound says the letter's name. Say the long-vowel sound for each letter. Trace the letter with your finger. Then write the letter on the line.

a   a   _____

e   e   _____

i   i   _____

o   o   _____

u   u   _____

Magic -e

Do you know there is a magic letter? A **magic -e** can change some short-vowel sounds into long-vowel sounds.
Add a **magic -e** to the end of each word below.
Write the new word on the line. Say the word aloud.

mad + e _____

can + e _____

hid + e _____

fin + e _____

cub + e _____

tub + e _____

Long -a

Sometimes more than one letter is needed to make a long-vowel sound. The **long -a** sound can be spelled with the letter **-a** and a **magic -e**, as in **plane**. It can also be spelled **-ai**, as in **train**. Look at each **long -a** word below. Sort the words by how they are spelled. Write each word in the correct column.

| aim | bake | late | mail | make |
| race | rain | sail | take | wait |

ai	a_e
_____	_____
_____	_____
_____	_____
_____	_____
_____	_____

Long -a

Woody and Buzz are in a **race**.

If you were in a **race**, what would your vehicle look like? Draw a picture of it.

Long -e

Read each **long -e** word aloud. Listen for the words that rhyme. Draw a line to match each pair of rhyming words.

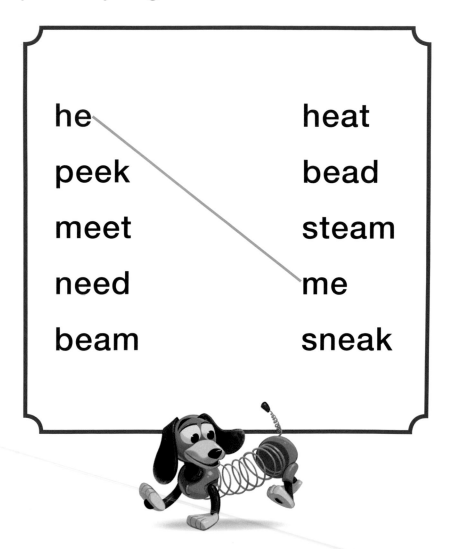

he	heat
peek	bead
meet	steam
need	me
beam	sneak

Long -e

Woody and Bo Peep make a great **team**.

You can help Woody and Bo Peep find Forky. Draw a line along the path with words that have the **long -e** sound.

START

bed · next · check · get

need · peek · keep · desk

free

be · let · he · help

left · key

them · we · swell · set · step

see

then · leave · well

when · meet

Rex is a **dinosaur**.
Dinosaur has a **long -i** sound.

Unscramble the letters to make words that have the **long -i** sound. Choose from the words in the box below. Write the words on the lines.

| find | hide | kind | like | ride | time |

eidh _ _ _ _

dfni _ _ _ _

nikd _ _ _ _

kiel _ _ _ _

miet _ _ _ _

drei _ _ _ _

Long -i

Woody and his friends are looking for clues.

Can you find the answers to the clues below?
Read the clues. Write the **long -i**
words in the correct boxes.

CLUES
1) **The opposite of dark**
2) **_ _ _ _ _ _-and-seek**
3) **We measure this with a clock.**

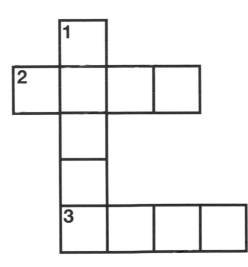

light   hide   time

Long -o

Read the words below aloud. Circle the words that have the **long -o** sound. Put an x on the words that do <u>not</u> have the **long -o** sound

no	go	got
hop	home	own
joke	poke	not
cold	on	gold
show	pony	trot
slow	know	stop

Long -o

Woody's **home** is with Andy. The word **home** has a **long -o** sound.

Draw a picture of your **home**.

Can you find the following **long -u** words in the puzzle below? Circle them.

cube	few	music	use
cute	huge	mute	view

R	E	F	E	W	S
Z	M	M	U	T	E
M	U	S	I	C	V
U	S	E	D	U	I
C	U	B	E	T	E
E	H	U	G	E	W

Long -u

The **long -u** sound can be spelled with the letter **-u** and a **magic -e**, as in **use**. It can also be spelled **-ew**, as in **few**. Look at each **long -u** word below. Sort the words by how they are spelled. Write each word in the correct column.

| cube | cute | few | huge | mew | new |

u_e

_____

_____

_____

ew

_____

_____

_____

Analogies

Analogies are logic puzzles that compare different things. You have to figure out how they are the same.

Complete each analogy by writing the correct word on the line. Choose from the **long-vowel** words in the box.

ate	go	huge	light	train

Sing is to **sang** as **eat** is to ___ate___.

Slow is to **fast** as **stop** is to _____.

Night is to **dark** as **day** is to _____.

Small is to **tiny** as **big** is to _____.

Road is to **car** as **tracks** are to

_____.

Long-Vowel Words

Sort the words below according to their **long-vowel** sounds. Write each word under the correct **long-vowel** sound.

dream	know	space	tie	use
joke	light	sweet	train	view

Long -a

_____

_____

Long -e

_____

_____

Long -i

_____

_____

Long -o

_____

_____

Long -u

_____

_____

Answers

Page 2

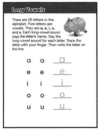

Long Vowels

There are 26 letters in the alphabet. Five letters are vowels. They are a, e, i, o, and u. Each long-vowel sound says the letter's name. Say the long-vowel sound for each letter. Trace the letter with your finger. Then write the letter on the line.

a	a	a
e	e	e
i	i	i
o	o	o
u	u	u

Page 3

Magic -e

Do you know there is a magic letter? A magic -e can change some short-vowel sounds into long-vowel sounds. Add a magic -e to the end of each word below. Write the new word on the line. Say the word aloud.

mad + e made
can + e cane
hid + e hide
fin + e fine
cub + e cube
tub + e tube

Page 4

Long -a

Sometimes more than one letter is needed to make a long-vowel sound. The long -a sound can be spelled with the letter -a and a magic -e, as in plane. It can also be spelled -ai, as in train. Look at each long -a word below. Sort the words by how they are spelled. Write each word in the correct column.

aim   bake   late   mail   make
race   rain   sail   take   wait

ai	a_e
aim	bake
mail	late
rain	make
sail	race
wait	take

Page 6

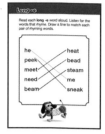

Long -e

Read each long -e word aloud. Listen for the words that rhyme. Draw a line to match each pair of rhyming words.

he — heat
peek — bead
meet — steam
need — me
beam — sneak

Page 7

Long -e

Woody and Bo Peep make a great team.

You can help Woody and Bo Peep find Forky. Draw a line along the path with words that have the long -e sound.

Page 8

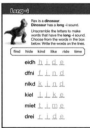

Long -i

Rex is a dinosaur. Dinosaur has a long -i sound.

Unscramble the letters to make words that have the long -i sound. Choose from the words in the box below. Write the words on the lines.

find   hide   kind   like   ride   time

eidh h i d e
dfni f i n d
nikd k i n d
kiel l i k e
miet t i m e
drei r i d e

Page 9

Long -i

Woody and his friends are looking for clues. Can you find the answers to the clues below? Read the clues. Write the long -i words in the crossword.

CLUES
1) The opposite of dark
2) ____-and-seek
3) We measure this with a clock.

Page 10

Long -o

Read the words below aloud. Circle the words that have the long -o sound. Put an x on the words that do not have the long -o sound.

no	go	lost
pop	home	own
joke	poke	not
cold	on	gold
show	pony	box
slow	know	stop

Page 12

Long -u

Can you find the following long -u words in the puzzle below? Circle them.

cube   few   music   use
cute   huge   mute   view

R	E	F	E	W	S
Z	M	M	U	T	E
M	U	S	I	C	V
U	S	E	D	U	I
C	U	B	E	T	E
E	H	U	G	E	W

Page 13

Long -u

The long -u sound can be spelled with the letter -u and a magic -e, as in use. It can also be spelled -ew, as in few. Look at each long -u word below. Sort the words by how they are spelled. Write each word in the correct column.

cube   cute   few   huge   mew   new

u_e	ew
cube	few
cute	mew
huge	new

Page 14

Analogies

Analogies are logic puzzles that compare different things. You have to figure out how they are the same.

Complete each analogy by writing the correct word on the line. Choose from the long-vowel words in the box.

ate   go   huge   light   train

Sing is to sang as eat is to   ate
Slow is to fast as stop is to   go
Night is to dark as day is to   light
Small is to tiny as big is to   huge
Road is to car as tracks are to   train

Page 15

Long-Vowel Words

Sort the words below according to their long-vowel sounds. Write each word under the correct long-vowel sound.

dream   know   space   tie   use
joke   light   sweet   train   view

Long -a	Long -e
space	dream
train	sweet

Long -i	Long -o
tie	know
light	joke

| Long -u |
| use |
| view |